HOLD ON
TO YOUR
PANTS

Gotham Books
30 N Gould St.
Ste. 20820, Sheridan, WY 82801
https://gothambooksinc.com/
Phone: 1 (307) 464-7800

Published by Gotham Books (date published Sep 1, 2021)

ISBN: 978-1-956349-00-9 (sc)
ISBN: 978-1-956349-01-6 (e)

Library of Congress Control Number: 2021916280

HOLD ON
TO YOUR
PANTS

Written by: Joseph L. Parsley

Illustrated by: Ben A. Parsley

Little girls like to put clothes on small animals. Imagine some of these animals escaping and taking their clothes with them.

This is a story poem about a make-believe Kallaboo animal family that feel like they need to wear pants but cannot make them stay up. If a Kallaboo were a real animal, they would probably get along well with people because we would see how cute they are, and we would try to help them keep their pants up. They may not even mind us laughing when their pants fall down.

If you take a Koala Bear and a Wallaroo,

And mix them both together, you get a Kallaboo.

It would be a Wallaroo with no tail that walks like you or me,
Or a Koala Bear that eats grass and cannot climb a tree.

You might not find a Kallaboo anywhere around,
But you will know it if you see it, cause their pants fall down.

Mama Kallaboo was sitting on the couch.
She said, "I can't do much with a baby in my pouch."

"If my baby had pants, he could follow me around,"
So, she put pants on him, and his pants fell down.

So, she sewed on a button, and it buttoned really good,
The button was working like she thought a button should.

She got the baby dressed so they could go to town,
But the button popped off, and his pants fell down.

She went into a store to see what she could find,
Baby Boo held up his pants and followed close behind.

There inside the store was a rag doll clown,

And when the baby reached to grab it, his pants fell down.

Now mama was thinking that suspenders might do,
Have you ever seen suspenders on a baby Kallaboo?

Baby Boo was laughing and hopping all around,

The suspenders popped off, and his pants fell down.

Then, mama tried a belt, and she got it too tight,
So, she loosened up the belt to try to get it right.

When she got it loose enough, to make the baby not frown,

The belt was too loose, and his pants fell down.

Now the baby saw something that looked like the moon,
Mama said, "that is a rainbow balloon."

She tied it to his pants, and he was prancing all around,
The balloon went "POP" and his pants fell down.

It popped him on his face, it was yucky sticky wet,
And Baby Boo was very-very-**VERY** upset.

The owner came running when he heard the loud sound,
Then he laughed so hard, it made his pants fall down.

Mama went back home with her baby in her pouch,
Daddy came home and found them sitting on the couch.

Coming in, he stumbled on the rag doll clown,
Then his hat flew off, and his pants fell down.

Different ones are different with different things to do,

Whether be a person or a Kallaboo.

HOLD ON TO YOUR PANTS as the Earth spins around,

'Cause gravity is trying to make your pants fall down!

About the Author

I came from a family of twelve children. I was born in Kentucky, raised in Illinois. I spent six years in the Army and am a Vietnam veteran. I met my wife in Fort Gordon, Georgia, where I was working as an Army drill Sargent. We have three sons and a daughter. Our youngest son was born with a birth defect and will always be at home with us. We now have five loving grandchildren. We still live in the same house in the country with twelve acres in north Alabama, that we moved into five years after we were married. We are still happy, healthy and enjoying life.

CPSIA information can be obtained
at www.ICGtesting.com
Printed in the USA
LVHW070433250821
696051LV00010B/313